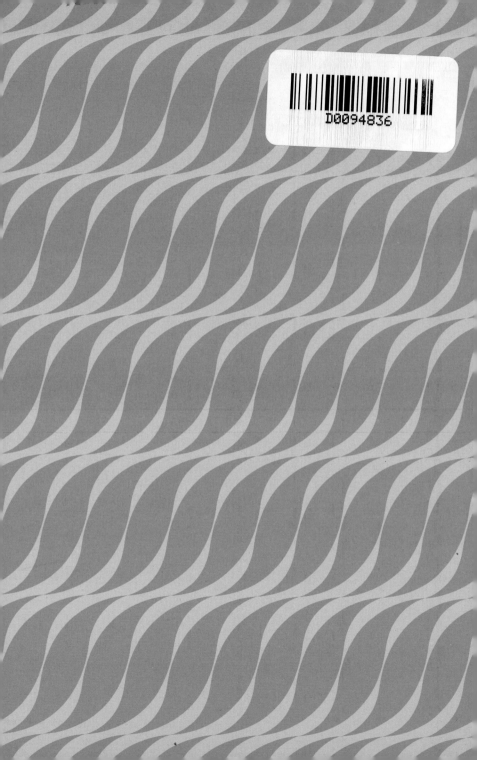

HOME
TILING

HOME
TILING

Mike Lawrence

southwater

This edition is published by Southwater

Distributed in the UK by
The Manning Partnership
251–253 London Road East
Batheaston
Bath BA1 7RL
tel. 01225 852 727
fax 01225 852 852

Published in the USA by
Anness Publishing Inc.
27 West 20th Street
Suite 504
New York
NY 10011
fax 212 807 6813

Distributed in Canada by
General Publishing
895 Don Mills Road
400–402 Park Centre
Toronto, Ontario M3C 1W3
tel. 416 445 3333
fax 416 445 5991

Distributed in Australia by
Sandstone Publishing
Unit 1, 360 Norton Street
Leichhardt
New South Wales 2040
tel. 02 9560 7888
fax 02 9560 7488

© Anness Publishing Limited 2001

10 9 8 7 6 5 4 3 2 1

Publisher: Joanna Lorenz
Managing Editor: Judith Simons
Art Manager: Clare Reynolds
Project Editor: Felicity Forster
Editor: Ian Penberthy
Photographer: John Freeman
Illustrator: Andrew Green
Designer: Bill Mason
Editorial Reader: Jonathan Marshall
Production Controller: Joanna King

ACKNOWLEDGEMENTS AND NOTES
The publisher would like to
thank The Tool Shop for supplying
tools for jacket photography:
97 Lower Marsh
Waterloo, London SE1 7AB
Tel 020 7207 2077; Fax 020 7207 5222
www.thetoolshop-diy.com

CONTENTS

INTRODUCTION

Tiles have a long pedigree in the interior decoration business. Faience (glazed earthenware) plaques have been found in Cretan buildings dating from around 1800 BC, and a tradition of ceramic wall and floor decoration was established soon after this farther east in Syria and Persia (now Iran). Mosaic wall and floor decorations, incorporating stone (usually marble), glass and ceramic tesserae, were a major feature of Roman interiors. The technique spread to North Africa and thence to Spain, and the Renaissance soon led to widespread use of decorative tiling all over Europe.

Probably the most important centre of ceramic tile making in Europe was Holland, where the creation of individually hand-painted tiles in a unique blue-grey colour soon made Delft famous in the early 17th century. From there, the use of tiles spread rapidly, and it was not long before mass production was introduced. The end product is the familiar ceramic tile we use today. The manufacturing and printing technology may have changed, and the adhesives and grouts used may have improved, but the result would be familiar to a 17th-century Dutchman.

The 20th century has brought new kinds of tile, notably vinyl, lino and cork tiles, which owe their existence to advances in plastics and resins technology. They offer a combination of properties that make them useful alternatives to ceramics in a wide range of situations, and generally are much less expensive.

This book concentrates on working with ceramic wall tiles, since they are the most popular of the types available. A wide range of situations is dealt with, from splashbacks to whole walls, including information on working around obstacles such as door and window openings and on creating special effects with tiled borders and feature panels. There are also sections on using other types of wall tiles, and on tiling floors.

ABOVE: Tile friezes and panels have been used to clad walls since the Renaissance, and can make a stunning focal point in a garden or courtyard.

LEFT, BELOW AND OPPOSITE: Tiles have never before been available in such a profusion of styles and designs. These range from highly glazed plain types to more rustic versions with matt or textured surfaces, and patterns that look as though they have been hand painted.

MATERIALS & EQUIPMENT

Ceramic tiles provide the most durable of all finishes in the home, whether for walls, floors or worktops, and there has never been a bigger choice of colours, designs, shapes and sizes. Vinyl, lino and cork floor tiles offer an alternative floor finish to ceramics, and offer the advantages of ease of laying combined with a surface finish that is warmer to the touch and also less noisy underfoot than ceramic tiles. For a hard-wearing and attractive floor, there are also quarry tiles, ideal for areas that receive a lot of foot traffic. For most tiling jobs, you will need tools for measuring, spacing and cutting the tiles, and adhesive and grout for attaching the tiles. Notched spreaders and grout finishers are usually sold with adhesives and grouts.

WALL TILES

In today's homes, the surfaces that are tiled more often than any other are walls, especially in rooms such as kitchens and bathrooms, where a hard-wearing, water-resistant and easy-to-clean decorative finish is required. Often the tiling protects only the most vulnerable areas such as splashbacks above wash basins and shower cubicles; but sometimes the whole room is tiled from floor to ceiling.

Tiles used for wall decoration are generally fairly thin, measuring from 4 to 6mm ($^3/_{16}$ to $^1/_4$in) thick, although some imported tiles (especially the larger sizes) may be rather thicker than this. The commonest kinds are square, measuring 108mm (4$^1/_4$in) or 150mm (6in) across, but rectangular tiles measuring 200 x 100mm (8 x 4in) and 200 x 150mm (8 x 6in) are becoming more popular.

Tile designs change with fashions in interior design, and current demand seems to be mainly for large areas of neutral or small-patterned tiles interspersed with individual motif tiles on a matching background. Plain tiles, often with a simple border frame, are also popular, as are tiles that create a frieze effect when laid alongside one another. Some sets of tiles build up into larger designs (known as feature panels), which can look quite striking when surrounded by an area of plain tiling.

The surface of ceramic wall tiles is no longer always highly glazed, as it was traditionally. Now there are semi-matt finishes, often with a slight surface texture that softens the harsh glare produced by a high-gloss surface.

Tile edges have changed over the years too. Once, special round-edged tiles were used for the exposed edges of tiled areas, and plain ones with unglazed square edges elsewhere. Nowadays, tiles are either the universal type or the standard square-edged variety. Both types usually have two adjacent edges glazed so they can be used as perimeter tiles, and sometimes all four edges are glazed.

LEFT: Wall tiles can be used to make eye-catching schemes, mixed geometrically or at random.

MOSAICS

Mosaics are just tiny tiles – usually plain in colour, sometimes with a pattern – that are sold made up in sheets on an open-weave cloth backing. These sheets are laid like larger tiles in a bed of adhesive, and all the gaps, including those on the surface of the sheet, are grouted afterwards. Square mosaics are the most common, but roundels, hexagons and other interlocking shapes are also available. Sheets are usually square and 300mm (12in) across, and are often sold in packs of five or ten. The best way of estimating quantities is to work out the area to be covered and to divide that by the coverage figure given on the pack to work out how many packs to buy. Note that wall and floor types are of different thicknesses, as with ordinary ceramic tiles.

ABOVE AND BELOW: Mosaic tiles are regaining the popularity they enjoyed in times past, but laying them is definitely a labour of love.

FLOOR TILES

Although less widely used than wall tiles, ceramic floor tiles are a popular choice for heavy traffic areas such as porches and hallways. They are generally thicker and harder-fired than wall tiles, to enable them to stand up to heavy wear without cracking. Again, a wide range of plain colours, simple textures and more elaborate designs is available. Common sizes are 150mm (6in) and 200mm (8in) squares and 200 x 100mm (8 x 4in) rectangles; hexagons are also available in plain colours, and a popular variation is a plain octagonal tile that is laid with small square coloured or decorated inserts at the intersections.

Quarry tiles are unglazed ceramic floor tiles with a brown, buff or reddish colour, and are a popular choice for hallways, conservatories and country-style kitchens. They are usually laid in a mortar bed, and after the joints have been grouted the tiles must be sealed with boiled linseed oil or a recommended proprietary sealer. Common sizes are 100mm (4in) and 150mm (6in) square. Special shaped tiles are also available for forming upstands at floor edges.

Terracotta tiles look similar to quarry tiles, but are larger and are fired at lower temperatures, so they are more porous. They are sealed in the same way as quarry tiles. Squares, ranging in size between 200 and 400mm (8 and 16in), and rectangles are the commonest shapes, but octagonal versions with small square in-fill tiles are also popular.

Cork tiles come in a small range of colours and textures. Their surface feels warm and relatively soft underfoot, and they also give some worthwhile heat and sound insulation – particularly

FAR LEFT: Ceramic floor tile with a painted medieval design.

MIDDLE: Ceramic tiles provide a durable and waterproof surface for bathroom floors.

LEFT: Quarry tiles provide a durable and attractive floor covering, and are especially suited to kitchens and conservatories.

useful in bathrooms, kitchens, halls and even children's bedrooms. The cheapest types have to be sealed to protect the surface after they have been laid, but the more expensive vinyl-coated floor types can be walked on as soon as they have been stuck down. They need little more than an occasional wash and polish to keep them in good condition. However, even the best cork floor tiles are prone to damage from sharp heels and heavy furniture, for example.

Vinyl tiles come in a very wide range of plain and patterned types, and generally resist wear better than cork, so they can be used on floors subject to fairly heavy wear. However, they are a little less gentle on the feet. Some of the more expensive types give very passable imitations of luxury floor coverings such as marble and terrazzo. Most are made in self-adhesive form and very little maintenance is needed once they have been laid.

Modern lino tiles, made from natural materials rather than the plastic resins used in vinyl tiles, offer far better performance than traditional linoleum. They come in a range of bright and subtle colours and interesting patterns, often with pre-cut borders.

All these types generally come in 300mm (12in) squares, although larger squares and rectangles are available in

ABOVE LEFT: Cork is the warmest of tiled floor coverings underfoot, and when sealed is good-looking and durable too.
MIDDLE: The more expensive types of vinyl floor tile offer superb imitations of other materials, such as wood, marble and terrazzo.
ABOVE RIGHT: Lino tiles offer a warm, attractive and durable alternative to cork and vinyl floor coverings in rooms such as kitchens and hallways.

some of the more expensive ranges. They are generally sold in packs of nine, covering roughly 0.84 sq m (1 sq yd), although many kinds are often available singly.

TOOLS

For almost any ceramic tiling job, large or small, the following tools are needed: some tile spacers; a steel tape measure; some lengths of 38 x 12mm (1½ x ½in) softwood battening (furring strips), plus masonry pins (tacks) and a hammer for supporting the tiles on large wall areas; a spirit level; a tile cutter; a tile saw; a tile file; a piece of dowel for shaping the grout lines or a proprietary grout shaper; a pencil and a felt-tip pen.

Tile cutters range from the basic – an angled cutting tip attached to a handle – to elaborate cutting jigs that guarantee perfectly accurate cuts every time. A tile saw is useful for making shaped cut-outs to fit around obstacles such as pipework, and a tile file or tile edge sander with abrasive strips helps to smooth cut edges.

Tile spacers are required when using standard field tiles. Other types have bevelled edges that create a grouting gap automatically when butted together. You can also create your own tile spacers with matchsticks (wooden matches) or strips of cardboard.

Tools needed for cork, vinyl and lino tiles are a tape measure, sharp utility knife and a steel straightedge for marking and cutting border tiles. A proprietary profile gauge with sliding steel or plastic needles makes it easy to cut tiles to fit around awkward obstacles such as architraves (trims) and pipework. But it is just as effective, and less costly, to cut a template from card or paper.

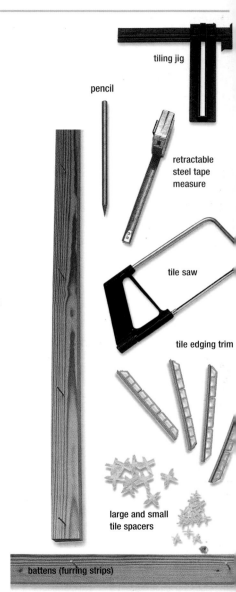

tiling jig

pencil

retractable
steel tape
measure

tile saw

tile edging trim

large and small
tile spacers

battens (furring strips)

spirit level

tile edge nippers

small tile files

tile scriber

tile cutter/ snapper

large tile files

tile edge sander with abrasive strips

hammer

heavy-duty tile cutter

dowel

masonry pins (tacks)

tile cutter with width and angle jig

homemade tile gauge

ADHESIVE AND GROUTING

Both adhesive and grout for wall tiling are now usually sold ready-mixed in plastic tubs complete with a notched plastic spreader. For areas that will get the occasional splash or may suffer from condensation, a water-resistant adhesive and grout is perfectly adequate, but for surfaces such as shower cubicles, which will have to withstand prolonged wetting, it is essential to use both waterproof adhesive and waterproof grout. Always use waterproof grout on tiled worktops; ordinary grout will harbour germs. Some silicone sealant or mastic (caulking) may also be needed for waterproofing joints where tiling abuts baths, basins and shower trays.

ADHESIVE

Ceramic floor tile adhesive is widely available in powder form as well as ready-mixed. It is best always to use a waterproof type (plus waterproof grout), even in theoretically dry areas.

Special water-based adhesive is the type to choose for both cork and lino tiles; solvent-based contact adhesives were formerly the first choice, but their fumes are extremely unpleasant and also dangerously inflammable, and they are no longer recommended. For vinyl-coated cork tiles, a special vinyl acrylic adhesive is needed. For vinyl tiles, an emulsion-type latex flooring adhesive is the best choice.

It is important that you allow adhesive to dry for at least 24 hours before applying grout.

GROUTING

Grout is generally white, but coloured grout is on sale and will make a feature of the grout lines (an effect that looks best with plain or fairly neutral patterned tiles).

Adhesive and grout are both sold in a range of quantities, sometimes labelled by weight, sometimes by volume; always check the coverage specified by the manufacturer on the packaging when buying, so as not to buy too much or run out halfway through the job.

TOOLS FOR ADHESIVE AND GROUTING

Notched spreaders are used for creating a series of ridges in the adhesive, allowing it to spread when the tile is pressed home, and ensuring that an even thickness of adhesive is applied. They are available in various sizes. Grouting tools include a grout spreader, grout finisher and grout remover.

OTHER MATERIALS

A damp sponge or cloth is needed to remove excess grout from the faces of the tiles, and a clean, dry cloth is needed to polish the tiles afterwards.

For protection, a face mask, safety goggles and leather gloves should be worn, especially when cutting and smoothing tiles, and when handling cut tiles. Rubber gloves should be worn when using tile adhesive, grout and grout colourant. If your skin is very sensitive, use a barrier cream also.

adhesive

small notched adhesive spreader

large notched adhesive spreader

grout finisher

grout

grout remover

grout spreader

polishing cloth

rubber gloves

sponge

RENEWING GROUT

Over the years, the grout in an existing tiled surface may become discoloured or cracked, which could cause serious problems in a shower. Fortunately, it can be renewed without having to strip off all the tiles. However, being very hard, it is difficult to remove and you will need a proper grout remover. This has a hardened, sharp serated blade.

If the grout is only discoloured, it can be removed to a depth of about 3mm ($\frac{1}{8}$in), then new grout applied on top; if it is cracked, however, go to the thickness of the tile before regrouting.

Take care when using a grout remover, as it may chip the glaze along the edges of the tiles, which will be difficult to disguise and may lead to water penetrating the tiled surface.

A grout remover is also useful for removing a damaged tile prior to replacing it. After raking out all the grout around the damaged tile, chip out the tile carefully with a hammer and cold chisel. Wear safety goggles and thick leather gloves to protect your eyes and hands from flying shards of tile, which will be sharp.

PLANNING & PREPARATION

The best way to practise tiling skills is to begin by covering just a small area such as a washbasin splashback, where setting out the tiles so that they are centred on the area concerned is a simple job, and there is very little tile cutting to do. For a larger area – a whole wall, or perhaps even a complete room – exactly the same techniques are used. The big difference is the sheer scale of the job, which makes the preliminary setting-out by far the most important part. The problem is that walls are seldom blank surfaces, and there may be a number of obstacles to tile around. Care must be taken to get the best fit with these inflexible tile squares, without needing to cut impossibly thin slivers to fill in gaps.

PLANNING

The most important thing to do is to plan precisely where the whole tiles will fall. On a flat, uninterrupted wall this is quite easy; simply find the centreline of the wall and plan the tiling to start from there. However, there will probably be obstacles such as window reveals, door openings and built-in furniture in the room, all competing to be the centre of attention, and it will be necessary to work out the best "centre-point" while all the time trying to avoid having very thin cut tile borders and edges.

It is best to use a device called a tiling gauge – a batten (furring strip) marked out in tile widths – to work this out. The gauge is easy to make from a straight piece of timber about 1.2m (4ft) long, marked off with pencil lines to match the size of the tile. Use this to ensure that the tiles will be centred accurately on major features such as window reveals, with a border of cut tiles of equal width at the end of each row or column of tiles.

The next stage is the actual setting-out. With large areas of tiling, two things are vitally important. First, the tile rows must be exactly horizontal; if they are not, errors will accumulate as the tiles extend across the wall, throwing the verticals out of alignment

with disastrous results. When tiling right around a room, inaccurate levels mean that rows will not match up at the start and finish points. Second, the tiles need some support while the adhesive sets; without it, they may slump down the wall.

The solution is to fix a line of battens across the wall – or right around the room – just above the level of the skirting (baseboard), securing them with partly-driven masonry nails (tacks) so that they can be removed later when the adhesive has set. The precise level will be dictated by setting-out with the tiling gauge, but usually will be between half and three-quarters of a tile width above the skirting. Do not rely on this being level; it may not be. Draw the line out in pencil first, using the spirit level, then pin the battens up and check the level again. If everything is straight, it is time to start tiling.

ESTIMATING QUANTITIES

When working out how many tiles you will need, first select the tile size. Then set out the area to be tiled on the wall and use the setting-out marks to count how many tiles are needed in each horizontal row and each vertical column. Count cut tiles as whole tiles, then multiply the two figures together to obtain the total required. Always add a further 5 per cent to the total to allow for breakages and miscalculations.

NUMBER OF TILES NEEDED

TILE SIZE	NO/SQ M	NO/SQ YD
108 x 108mm (4¼ x 4¼in)	86	71
200 x 100mm (8 x 4in)	48	41
150 x 150mm (6 x 6in)	43	36

MAKING AND USING A TILING GAUGE

1 Use a pencil and one of the chosen tiles to mark up a length of wood for use as a tiling gauge. Allow for the width of tile spacers if they are to be used.

2 Hold the tiling gauge horizontally against the wall to see how many tiles each row will take, and also to centre the tiling on a wall feature or window opening.

3 Similarly, hold the gauge vertically to assess how many tiles will fill each column, and where best to position any cut tiles that may be needed at top or bottom.

SETTING OUT TILED WALLS

Careful setting-out is essential to the success of any tiling job. The object is to obtain a balanced look to each tiled surface, with the rows of tiles being centred on the wall itself or on some prominent feature, much like you would centre a wallpaper pattern. This will ensure that any cut tiles at the margins or around a feature are of equal size.

Doors and window openings particularly can cause problems and often require quite a bit of thought.

TILING AROUND A DOOR

1 If the door is close to the room corner, start with whole tiles next to the frame. Use a vertical tile guide if the architrave (trim) is not truly vertical (it may not be).

2 Tile the whole of the main wall area, adding cut tiles next to the room corner and at ceiling level. Remove the tile supports when the adhesive has had time to set.

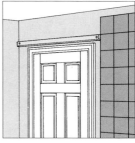

3 Fit a tile support above the door, in line with the tile rows, and another between it and the other room corner, just above skirting (baseboard) level.

4 Carry on placing whole tiles above the door opening, filling in with cut tiles at the room corner and at ceiling level, as in step 2.

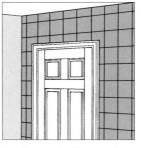

5 Remove the tile support above the door opening and fill in all around it with cut and whole tiles as required. Grout the tiles when the adhesive has set.

6 If the door opening is near or at the centre of the wall, centre the tiling on it and fix tile support battens (furring strips) as required.

TILING AROUND A WINDOW

1 For tiling a wall with a window opening, first decide on where to centre the tiling. On a wall with one window, centre the tiling on a line drawn through its centre.

2 If there are two window openings in a wall, centre the tiles on a line drawn through the centre of each window, provided an exact number of whole tiles will fit between them.

3 Otherwise, centre the tiling on a line drawn midway between the windows. Always work across and up the wall, placing whole tiles up to window-sill level, then up the wall at each side of the window. Fit a tile support above the opening to support whole tiles there.

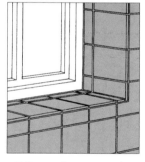

4 Remove the support strips and cut tiles to fit on the face wall at each side and across the top of the window. To tile a window reveal, place whole tiles so they overlap the edges of the tiles on the wall face. Then fill in between these and the frame with cut tiles.

POSITIONING CUT TILES FOR PANELS

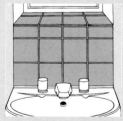

If the height of a tiled splashback is determined by a feature such as a mirror or window, position a row of cut tiles along the top of the panel. Make sure their top edges are overlapped by any tiles in a window recess.

If the width of the tiling is defined, as with a bath panel, always position cut tiles of equal size at each side.

SETTING OUT TILED FLOORS

Tiled floors need careful setting-out if the end result is to look neat and professional. This is especially important with glazed ceramic and quarry tiles and also patterned vinyl and lino tiles, but matters rather less with plain vinyl or cork tiles where the finished effect is of uniform colour and the joints between the tiles are practically invisible.

Fortunately the necessary setting-out is much easier with floor tiles than wall tiles, since the tiles can be dry-laid on the floor surface and moved around until a starting point is found that gives the best arrangement, with cut border tiles of approximately equal size all around the perimeter of the room.

In a regularly shaped room, start by finding the centre-point of the floor by linking the midpoints of opposite pairs of walls with string lines. In an irregularly shaped room, place string lines as shown in step 2 so that they avoid obstructions, then link the midpoints of opposite pairs of strings to find the room's centre. Now dry-lay rows of tiles out toward the walls in each direction, allowing for any joint thickness, to see how many whole tiles will fit in and to check whether this results in over-narrow border tiles or awkward cuts against obstacles. Move the rows slightly to improve the fit if necessary, then chalk the string lines and snap them against the floor to mark the starting point.

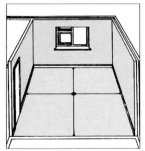

1 In a regularly shaped room, find the centre by linking the midpoints of opposite pairs of walls with string lines.

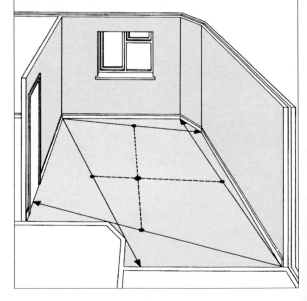

2 In an irregularly shaped room, use string lines that avoid obstacles, and link their midpoints to find the centre.

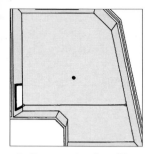

3 To ensure that tiles will be laid square to the door threshold if the walls are out of square, place a string line at right angles to the door opening across the room to the opposite wall.

4 Place a second string line at right angles to the first so that it passes through the room's centre-point.

5 Place a third string line at right angles to the second, again passing through the centre-point, to complete the laying guide.

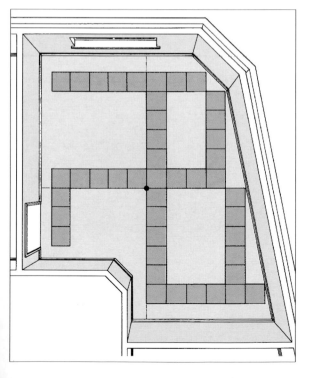

6 Dry-lay rows of tiles out from the centre of the room toward the walls, allowing for the joint width, as appropriate, to determine the width of the border tiles and the fit of the tiles around any obstacles.

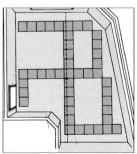

7 Adjust the string lines to obtain the best possible fit, chalk them and snap them against the floor to mark the laying guidelines.

PREPARING A SURFACE FOR TILING

The surface for tiling should be clean and dry. It is possible to tile over painted plaster or plasterboard (gypsum board), but old wall coverings should be removed and brick walls must be rendered. Note that modern tile adhesives allow tiling over existing tiles, so there is no need to remove these if they are securely bonded to the wall surface. There is also no need to fill minor cracks or holes; the tile adhesive will bridge these as it is applied to the wall surface. Printed wallpaper can easily be removed because it will absorb water splashed on it immediately; other types will not. With paper-backed fabric wall coverings, it is often possible to peel the fabric away from its paper backing; try this before turning to other methods.

REMOVING WALLPAPER

1 To strip printed wallpaper, wet the surface with a sponge or a garden spray gun. Wait for the water to penetrate, and repeat if necessary.

WASHING WALLS AND CEILINGS

Wash wall surfaces down with sugar soap (all-purpose cleaner) or detergent, working from the bottom up, then rinse them with clean water, working from the top down. Wash ceilings with a floor mop or squeegee, after disconnecting and removing light fittings. Again, rinse off with clean water.

4 After removing the bulk of the old wallpaper, go back over the wall surface and remove any remaining "nibs" of paper with sponge/spray gun and scraper.

2 Using a stiff wallpaper scraper – not a filling knife (putty knife) – start scraping the old paper from the wall at a seam. Wet it again while working if necessary.

3 Turn off the power before stripping around switches and other fittings, then loosen the faceplate screws to strip the wallpaper behind them.

5 To strip a washable wallpaper, start by scoring the plastic coating with a serrated scraper or toothed roller, then soak and scrape as before.

6 For quicker results, use a steam stripper to remove washable papers. Press the steaming plate to the next area while stripping the area just steamed.

TILING
TECHNIQUES

Tiling is relatively straightforward and does not require a lot of expensive equipment. It pays to plan each tiling project carefully and not to rush it. The more you practise, the more skilled you will become – tiling the walls or floor of a whole room is too large an undertaking for a beginner, but tiling a skirting board (baseboard), window recess or splashback can be accomplished after only a little experience. Having thoroughly prepared the surface to be tiled, you will need to work quite quickly, as the adhesive and grout will begin to go off quite rapidly. Tackle small sections at a time, cleaning off any excess as you go before it has a chance to harden. This is particularly important with combined adhesives and grouts.

BEGINNING TO TILE

FITTING TILE SUPPORTS

Use masonry pins (tacks) to fix the support to the wall, aligned with the guideline. Drive the pins in only part of the way so that they can be pulled out to remove the batten (furring strip) later.

When tiling large areas or whole walls, pin a vertical guide batten to the wall as well to help keep the tile columns truly vertical.

FIXING TILES

Once all the necessary setting-out work has been done, the actual technique of fixing tiles to walls is quite simple: spread the adhesive and press the tiles into place. However, there must be an adhesive bed of even thickness to ensure that neighbouring tiles sit flush with one another. To obtain this, use a toothed spreader (usually supplied with the tile adhesive; buy one otherwise). Scoop some adhesive from the tub with the spreader, and draw it across the wall with the teeth pressed hard against the plaster to leave ridges of a standard height on the wall. Apply enough adhesive to fix about ten or twelve tiles at a time.

Bed the tiles into the adhesive with a pressing and twisting motion, aligning the first tile with the vertical guideline or batten. If using tile spacers, press one into the adhesive next to the top corner of the first tile, and place the second tile in the row.

MARKING OUT A SPLASHBACK

1 When tiling a small area with rows of whole tiles, use the tiling gauge to mark the extent of the tiled area on the wall. Here each row will have five tiles.

Carry on placing spacers and tiles until the end of the row is reached. Add subsequent rows in the same way until all the whole tiles are in place.

2 Next, use a spirit level to mark a true horizontal base line, above which the first row of whole tiles will be fixed. Cut tiles will fit below it.

3 Then use the spirit level again to complete a grid of horizontal and vertical guidelines on the wall surface, ready for a wooden tile support to be fixed.

FIXING TILES

1 Use a notched spreader to spread adhesive on the wall. Press the teeth against the wall to leave ridges of even height. Place the first tile on the tile support, with its side against the pencilled guideline or vertical guide batten (furring strip).

2 Insert a tile spacer at the tile corner and place the second tile. Add more tiles to complete the row, then build up succeeding rows in the same way.

CUTTING TILES

It is now time to tackle any cut tiles that are needed at the ends of the rows, and along the base of the tiled area beneath the horizontal tile support. Remove this, and the tile spacers, only when the adhesive has set; allow 24 hours.

When cutting border tiles, measure each cut tile individually at top and bottom or each side as necessary. The walls, floors and ceilings of houses are rarely true and you are likely to find that the gaps to be filled will vary from one tile to the next. Straight cuts can be made with a small cutter or cutting jig, while shapes will need to be nibbled out with nippers or cut with a tile saw.

1 Use a pencil-type tile cutter and a straightedge to make straight cuts. Measure and mark the tile width needed, then score a line across the glaze.

4 The traditional way of making a cut-out in a tile is to score its outline on the tile, then gradually nibble away the waste material with pincers or tile nippers.

5 An alternative is to use a special abrasive-coated tile saw. This is indispensable for making cut-outs – to fit around pipes and similar obstructions.

2 Place a nail or matchstick (wooden match) under the scored line at each side of the tile, and break it with downward hand pressure on each half of the tile.

3 Use a cutting guide or tiling jig if preferred, especially for cutting narrow strips. This type holds the tile securely and also guides the tile cutter accurately.

USING A TILE-CUTTING JIG

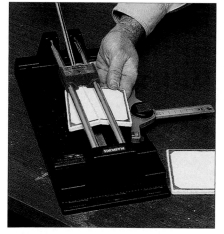

1 For making angled cuts as well as straight ones, a tile-cutting jig is invaluable. To set it up, first fix the side fence to the angle required.

2 Draw the cutting point across the tile, scoring the tile only once. Snap the tile by holding it against the guide bars and lowering the cutter handle with its tip under the tile.

ADDING CUT TILES

When tiling a whole wall, cut tiles are likely to be needed at the corners at each end of the wall, and at the skirting (base) board and ceiling. If the tiling is to extend on to an adjacent wall, the horizontal rows must align, so extra care is needed when setting out.

At an internal corner, tile up to the angle completely on one wall so that its tiles overlap the edges of the tiles on the first wall. You can do the same thing at an external corner, using glazed-edge tiles on one wall to conceal the edges of the tiles on the other, provided the angle is truly vertical. If it is not, bed corner strip in the adhesive, set it vertical, then tile up to it.

1 Measure, mark and cut the sections of tile needed to complete each row of tiling. Spread a little adhesive over their backs and press them into place.

2 When tiling adjacent walls, place all the cut pieces on the first wall. Repeat on the second, overlapping the original cut pieces. If cut tiles are only needed on one wall, make sure they are overlapped by the whole tiles on the adjacent wall.

3 When tiling external corners, set out the tiles so that, if possible, whole tiles meet on the corner. Overlap the tiles as shown, or to fit plastic corner trim.

GROUTING

When all the tiles are in place, including any cut tiles that are required, it is time to tackle the final stage of the job – filling in the joint lines between the tiles with grout. You should leave adhesive to dry for at least 24 hours before grouting. Ready-mixed grout is a little more expensive than powdered, but more convenient to use. You need a flexible spreader (usually supplied with the grout) to force the grout into the gaps, a damp sponge or cloth to remove excess grout from the faces of the tiles, and a short length of wooden dowel or a proprietary grout shaper to smooth the grout lines. A, clean, dry cloth will be needed to polish the tiles afterwards.

1 Apply the grout to the tile joints by drawing the loaded spreader across them at right angles to the joint lines. Scrape off excess grout and reuse it.

2 Use a damp sponge or cloth to wipe the surface of the tiles before the grout dries out. Rinse it in clean water from time to time.

3 Then use a short length of wooden dowel or a similar tool to smooth the grout lines to a gentle concave cross-section. Allow the grout to harden completely, then polish the tiles with a dry cloth to remove any remaining bloom.

ALTERNATIVE EDGING TECHNIQUES

Most ceramic wall tiles have two glazed edges, making it possible to finish off an area of tiling or an external corner with a glazed edge exposed. However, there are alternative ways of finishing off tiling. It can be edged with wooden mouldings or plastic trim strips.

Wooden mouldings can be bedded into the tile adhesive on walls; to edge worktops they can be pinned (tacked) or screwed to the worktop edge.

Plastic edge and corner mouldings (nosings) have a perforated flange that is bedded in the tile adhesive before the tiles are placed. These mouldings come in a range of pastel and bright primary colours to complement or contrast with the tiling. Take care when fitting them to make sure they are vertical, checking with a spirit level, otherwise they will cause problems when you come to add the tiles. Remember to allow a grouting gap between the moulding and the tiles.

Another method of finishing off the edge of a tiled area is to use proprietary border tiles. These are special narrow tiles that come in a variety of widths, normally coinciding with standard tile widths, and usually have a glazed edge that can be exposed. Border tiles offer a wide range of patterns to choose from, and some even have moulded relief patterns for added interest. They can be used horizontally or vertically.

ABOVE: Bed plastic edge or corner trim into the adhesive, then position the tiles so that they fit flush against the curved edge of the trim strip.

EDGING A COUNTER TOP

1 Wood can be used to edge a tiled counter top. Start by attaching the moulding to the edge of the worktop so it will fit flush with the tiled surface. Mitre the ends of the lengths of moulding to produce neat internal and external corners.

ABOVE: As an alternative to plastic, use wooden mouldings bedded in the tile adhesive. Here, an L-shaped moulding forms a neat external corner trim.

ABOVE: When tiling over existing tiles, some way of disguising the double thickness along exposed edges will be needed. A quadrant (quarter-round) moulding is ideal.

2 Spread the tile adhesive and bed the tiles in place, checking that they lie level with the top edge of the moulding and flush with each other.

3 Plug the counter-bored screw holes by gluing in short lengths of dowel and chiselling them off flush with the moulding. Sand them smooth. Finally, grout the tile joints for a neat finish and paint, stain or varnish the mouldings.

LAYING CERAMIC FLOOR TILES

Both glazed ceramic and quarry tiles can be laid directly over a concrete floor, as long as it is sound and dry. They can also be laid on a suspended timber floor if it is strong enough to support the not inconsiderable extra weight (check this with a building surveyor). In this case, cover the floorboards with exterior-grade plywood, screwed down or secured with annular nails (spiral flooring nails) to prevent it from lifting; this will provide a stable, level base for the tiles.

Glazed ceramic floor tiles are laid with specially formulated adhesive, which should be a waterproof type in bathrooms and a flexible type if tiling on a suspended floor. Quarry and terracotta tiles are laid on mortar over a solid concrete floor, and in thick-bed tile adhesive over plywood.

Old floor coverings should be lifted before laying ceramic or quarry tiles, but if a solid floor is covered with well-bonded vinyl or cork tiles, these can be left in place and tiled over, using tile adhesive. First remove any wax polish used on them.

Set out the floor as described previously, but transfer the starting point to the corner of the room farthest from the door once the setting-out has been completed.

1 Pin tiling guides to the floor in the corner of the room at right angles to each other, then spread some adhesive on the floor with a notched-edge trowel.

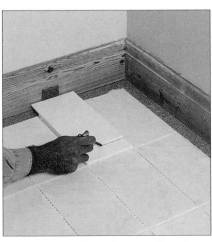

4 To cut border tiles to the correct size and shape, lay a whole tile over the last whole tile laid, butt another against the skirting (baseboard) and mark where its edge overlaps the tile underneath.

2 Place the first tile in the angle between the tiling guides, butting it tightly against them and pressing it down firmly into the adhesive bed.

3 As the tiles are laid, use the spacers to ensure an even gap between them. Use a straightedge and spirit level to check that all the tiles are horizontal.

5 Cut the marked tile and use the cut-off piece to fill the border gap. Repeat step 4, using the same tile until it becomes too narrow to fill the border gap.

6 Spread grout over the tiles to fill all the joint lines. Wipe excess grout from the surface of the tiles with a damp cloth. Use a piece of dowel or similar rounded tool to smooth the grout. Polish the tile with a clean, dry cloth.

LAYING QUARRY TILES

Quarry tiles offer a hard-wearing floor surface, which is ideal for areas that will receive a lot of foot traffic such as hallways. However, they are quite thick, which makes them difficult to cut, so consider carefully where you want to use them; an area that requires a lot of cut tiles may be impractical. Some suppliers will offer to cut quarry tiles for you, which can solve the problem. However, make sure you measure them carefully and mark them clearly.

As with tiling a wall, guide battens (furring strips) will be needed and should be nailed to the floor in one corner, making sure they make a right angle. Their thickness should be about double the thickness of the tiles to allow for the mortar on which the tiles are bedded.

When laying the tiles, it is necessary to work in bays so that the mortar thickness can be kept uniform. This is achieved by nailing a third batten to the floor parallel with one of the other two and four tile widths away from it. Then a board is cut as a spreader for the mortar, with notched ends that fit over the parallel battens so that an even thickness of mortar is achieved as the board is drawn along them. This should be the thickness of a tile plus 3mm (⅛in).

Before laying the tiles, soak them in a bucket of water, as this will prevent them from sucking all the moisture out of the mortar and weakening it.

1 Add a third tiling guide to form a bay four tiles wide. Put down a thin mortar bed and place the first row of tiles, using a tiling gauge to space them.

4 Complete the second bay in the same way as the first. Continue in this fashion across the room until all the whole tiles are laid. Allow the mortar to harden so that you can walk on the tiles before finally removing the guide battens.

2 Complete four rows of four tiles, then check that they are level. Tamp down any that are proud, and lift and re-bed any that are lying low.

3 Complete the first bay, then remove the third tiling guide and reposition it another four tile widths away. Fill the second bay with mortar and tamp it down.

5 If installing a tiled upstand, place this next, aligning individual units with the floor tiling. Then cut and fit the border tiles.

6 Mix up a fairly dry mortar mix and use a stiff-bristled brush to work it well into the joints between the tiles. Brush away excess mortar while working before it has a chance to harden, otherwise it will stain the faces of the tiles.

VINYL, LINO AND CORK FLOOR TILES

Vinyl, lino and cork floor tiles are available in both plain and self-adhesive types. Cork tiles may be unsealed or vinyl-coated. For plain vinyl tiles, an emulsion-type latex flooring adhesive is used, while plain cork tiles and lino tiles are best stuck with a water-based contact adhesive. For vinyl-coated cork tiles, use a special vinyl acrylic adhesive.

Since these tiles are comparatively thin, any unevenness in the sub-floor will show through the tiles. Cover timber floors with a hardboard underlay first. Concrete floors may need localized repairs or treatment with a self-smoothing compound.

If laying patterned tiles, set the floor out carefully. With plain tiles, setting out may not appear to be so important, but nevertheless the floor should still be set out carefully to ensure that the tile rows run out at right angles from the door.

1 If using self-adhesive tiles, simply peel the backing paper off and place the tile in position on the sub-floor against the marked guidelines.

2 Align self-adhesive tiles carefully before sticking them down; the adhesive grabs positively and repositioning may be difficult.

3 If using non-adhesive tiles, spread the appropriate type of adhesive on the sub-floor, using a notched spreader to ensure that an even thickness is applied.

4 After laying an area of tiles, use a smooth block of wood to work along the joints, pressing them down. This will ensure that they are all bedded firmly in the adhesive.

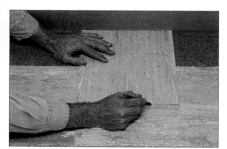

5 At the border, lay a tile over the last tile laid, butt another against the skirting (baseboard) and mark its edge on the tile underneath.

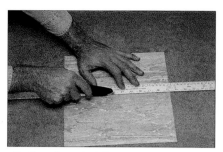

6 Place the marked tile on a board and cut it with a sharp knife. The exposed part of the sandwiched tile in step 5 will fit the gap perfectly.

7 Fit the cut piece of border tile in place. Trim its edge slightly if it is a tight fit. Mark, cut and fit the other border tiles in exactly the same way.

8 At an external corner, lay a whole tile over the last whole tile in one adjacent row, butt another against the wall and draw along its edge.

9 Move the sandwiched tile to the other side of the corner, again butt the second whole tile against the wall and mark its edge on the sandwiched tile.

10 Use the utility knife to cut out the square waste section along the marked lines, and offer up the L-shaped border tile to check its fit before fixing it.

USING CORK WALL TILES

Cork wall tiles are usually sliced into squares – 300mm (12in) is the commonest size – or rectangles. They come in a range of natural shades, and may also be stained or printed with surface designs during manufacture. They are stuck to the wall surface with a special water-based contact adhesive, and since they are virtually impossible to remove once placed, they should be regarded as a long-term decorative option and their use carefully planned.

Cork tiles are not rigid like ceramic wall tiles and will follow the contours of the wall, so it is essential that this is prepared properly before the tiles are applied. The surface must be sound and as flat as possible, with all major cracks and holes filled and sanded down.

As with ceramic tiles, careful setting out will allow you to minimize the amount of cutting required, although this is not as difficult as cutting rigid tiles – a sharp knife is all that is required. To avoid problems of slight colour changes between batches of tiles, mix them all thoroughly before beginning.

TIP
If using cork tiles on walls, change the faceplate screws on light switches and socket outlets (receptacles) for longer ones; the originals may be too short to reach the lugs in the mounting box.

1 To ensure that the tile rows and columns build up correctly, draw horizontal and vertical pencil guidelines on the wall. Place the first tile.

4 Fit the cut piece of border tile in place on the wall. Shave or sand its cut edge down a fraction if it is a tight fit. Cut and fit others in the same way until you have filled all the border areas completely.

2 If border tiles are to be cut, hold a whole tile over the last whole tile fixed, butt another against the frame and mark where its edge overlaps the tile underneath it.

3 Place the marked tile on a board and cut it with a sharp utility knife. The exposed part of the sandwiched tile in step 2 should fit the border gap precisely.

5 To fit a tile around an obstacle such as a light switch, make a paper or card template and test its fit before cutting the actual tile.

6 Run a kitchen rolling pin or a length of broom handle over the completed cork surface to ensure that all the tiles are well bonded to the wall, paying particular attention to the joints between tiles.

USING MOSAIC TILES

Small mosaic tiles are an attractive alternative to square and rectangular tiles, especially for small areas of tiling where their size will look particularly appropriate. Modern mosaic tiles come in a range of shapes and sizes, from simple squares and roundels to interlocking shapes such as hexagons. They are generally sold in sheets backed with an open-mesh cloth that holds the individual mosaic pieces at the correct spacing and greatly speeds up the installation process, since the entire sheet is stuck to the wall in one go. If cut pieces are needed to fill in the perimeter of the tiled area, simply cut individual mosaic tiles from the sheet with scissors, trim them to size with a tile cutter and position them one by one. Mosaic tiles are fixed and grouted with ordinary tiling products.

1 Start by putting up a horizontal tile support and a vertical tiling guide, as for ordinary tiling. Then apply an area of tile adhesive to the wall.

CUTTING MOSAIC TILES

As well as using sheets of tiles, you can create mosaics with tesserae. Small pieces of tile can be shaped with mosaic nippers: wearing protective leather gloves and safety goggles, place the jaws of the nippers at right angles to the tile and press them together to make a clean cut. Clear away small, sharp shards of tile immediately and dispose of them safely. Alternatively, wrap each tile separately in heavy sacking and place on a wooden cutting board. Wearing protective leather gloves and safety goggles, tap the tile smartly several times with a hammer. Unwrap carefully and dispose immediately of small, unusable shards.

2 Position the first sheet of mosaic tiles on the wall, in the angle between the tiling support and the tiling guide, and press it firmly into place.

3 After placing several sheets, use a mallet and a piece of plywood to tamp the mosaics down evenly. Use a towel or a thin carpet offcut as a cushion. Ensure the grouting spaces between each sheet are equal.

4 To fill in the perimeter of the area, snip individual mosaic tiles from the sheet, cut them to the size required and bed them firmly in the adhesive.

5 When the adhesive has dried, spread grout over the tiled area, working it well into the gaps between the individual mosaics. Wipe off excess grout with a damp sponge, and polish the surface with a cloth when dry.

TILING A WINDOW RECESS

Tiling a small area of a room will focus attention and add colour and pattern without being overpowering. Here, two different designs of hand-painted tiles have been used to accentuate a window recess, the colours complementing the bright-coloured wall.

For a completely different effect, plain terracotta tiles with curved edges would give a Mediterranean look to the window. Plain, matt-glazed tiles in rich shades of blue would create a very different note of Moorish magnificence.

Before you begin, measure the window recess carefully to determine how many tiles you will need. Allow a whole tile for each cut one to be on the safe side.

1 Wearing a face mask and gloves, sand the paintwork on the window sill and walls to remove any loose paint. Key (scuff) the surface to provide a base for the adhesive.

4 Place the first two tiles in position on the wall, butting them closely together and lining up the outside edge of the outer tile with the edge of the wall. Hold the tiles in place with masking tape until set. If the recess is less than two whole tiles deep, place the cut tiles next to the window frame.

2 Wearing rubber gloves, spread a thick layer of tile adhesive in one corner of the window. Using a damp sponge, remove any adhesive that gets on to the wall.

3 Using the notched edge of the spreader, key the surface only halfway through, leaving a thick layer of adhesive.

5 Spread adhesive in the opposite corner of the window and key as before. Position two vertical tiles as in step 4. Lay tiles along the window sill, overlapping the edges of the vertical tiles at each end.

6 Spread adhesive up the sides of the window recess and key. Position the contrasting tiles, lining up the edges with the edges of the recess. Tape in place as before until set. Grout all the tiles, removing any excess with a damp sponge. Polish with a dry, lint-free cloth.

TILING A DOOR PANEL

During the Victorian era, tiles were used to decorate all types of domestic objects, from fireplace surrounds to furniture. This idea has been adapted from the Victorian use of decorative panels to brighten up traditional interior doors. Once grouted, the edges of the tiles are encased with strips of thin wooden moulding. This provides a neat finish, echoing the design of the door panels, and helps to keep the tiles in place. Remember that tiles will make the door heavy, so the idea is not suitable for a child's room. Before you proceed, check that the door hinges are firmly attached and reinforce them if necessary.

1 Wearing a protective mask and gloves, prepare the surface of the door panels by rubbing them down with sandpaper.

4 Using a notched spreader, key (scuff) the surface of the adhesive to ensure good adhesion for the tiles.

2 Once the door is sanded, use a utility knife to score the panels, creating a key (scuffed surface) for the tile adhesive.

3 Wearing rubber gloves, spread a generous layer of flexible tile adhesive over the surface of the first door panel.

5 Position the tiles in order on the panel, using tile spacers if necessary. Remove excess adhesive using a damp sponge. Repeat the process to apply tiles to the other panels. Leave the adhesive to dry.

6 Grout the tiles. Remove the excess grout using a damp sponge and polish the tiles with a dry, lint-free cloth. Wearing a protective mask, cut strips of recessed moulding to fit around the panels, mitring the edges. Fix the moulding in position using panel pins (tacks). To prevent it from splitting, drill holes for the pins.

TILING A WORK SURFACE

This cheerful work surface or table top is a good way to use up an odd assortment of left-over tiles. The vibrant mix of colours creates the mood of a Mediterranean café. Because the tiles are not exactly the same size the spacing and grouting are judged by eye, but a little unevenness will add to the rustic charm!

Tiles for work surfaces need to be at least 6mm (¼in) thick to withstand heat, so normal wall tiles are not suitable. Choose tiles that are not too highly glazed, otherwise they will be very slippery and impractical to work on. Make sure the kitchen unit or table will bear the weight of the tiles by adding extra supports and strengthening the joints if necessary.

1 Measure your work unit or table top. Wearing a face mask, cut a piece of waterproof plywood or chipboard to fit. Seal both sides with PVA (white) glue and leave to dry.

4 Wearing rubber gloves, spread tile adhesive over the board. (If you need to cut tiles, start within the marked box.) Key (scuff) the surface of the adhesive using the notched edge of a spreader.

2 Lay the tiles on the board and work out the design. If you need to cut tiles to fit, find the centre of the board first and calculate the number of whole tiles. Draw a box around the area filled by the whole tiles.

3 Wearing a face mask, cut four battens (furring strips). Using panel pins (tacks), attach a batten to each side of the board so that they protrude above the edge to form a lip the same depth as the tiles.

5 Carefully position the tiles on the board, judging the grouting distance by eye. If necessary, cut tiles to fit. When the whole board has been tiled, remove excess adhesive with a damp sponge. Leave to set.

6 Apply the grout, following the manufacturer's instructions. Remove excess grout with a damp sponge, then polish the tiles with a dry, lint-free cloth.

DECORATIVE LAYOUTS

The preceding pages have dealt with tiling walls in the technical sense of planning the layout and fixing the tiles. However, tiles are more than just wall covering units; they come in a range of sizes and designs that can also be used creatively in a variety of ways. Tile manufacturers offer a range of mass-produced designs you can choose from, which can be used to great effect with the application of a little imagination, or you can select from a variety of unique hand-painted tiles available from better tile suppliers, antique tiles from salvage companies, or even commission a motif panel from a specialist tile supplier. Plan the motif's position on the wall carefully, and build it in the usual way as tiling progresses.

CHECKED PATTERN

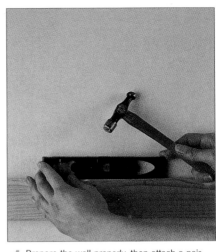

If you have your heart set on a particular tile, but find it is outside your budget, do not despair; you can create quite dramatic results with the cheapest of tiles as long as you use them imaginatively. Here, basic wall tiles in two shades of blue have been used to create a stunning chequerboard effect that is topped with a thin, decorative band of tile strips. The strips make a visual "dado rail" (chair rail) that divides the tiles' surface quite naturally into two distinct areas. The upper portion of the wall is then finished using lighter blue tiles. The strips can be cut from ordinary tiles, or use proper dado tiles.

1 Prepare the wall properly, then attach a pair of batten (furring strip) guides at right angles where the first row of tiles will start.

4 Lay the light coloured tiles in place above the border, using tile spacers as before. Cut any tiles you need to complete the edges and set them in place. Use a damp sponge to remove any excess adhesive and leave to dry.

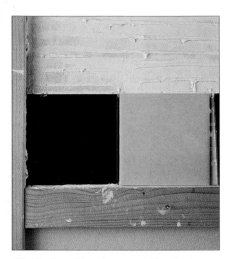

2 Wearing rubber gloves, apply tile adhesive using a notched spreader to key (scuff) the surface. Position the tiles, alternating light and dark.

3 When you have laid as many tiles as you want, cut 5cm (2in) strips of the darker tiles. Apply and key the tlle adhesive as before, then set the strips in position using tile spacers.

5 When the adhesive has set, grout the tiles thoroughly, wearing rubber gloves. Press the grout down into the gaps between the tiles.

6 Remove any excess grout using a damp sponge and leave to dry. When the grout has set, polish the surface of the tiles with a dry, lint-free cloth.

GEOMETRIC CHEQUERBOARD

Shades of blue and ivory Venetian glass tiles make a lovely cool splashback for a bathroom basin. They are arranged here in a simple geometric design, but you can experiment with other patterns – position the tiles diagonally to make a diamond shape, or use alternate coloured squares like a chequerboard.

For a co-ordinated look, use one of the tile colours to make a thin border around the bath or repeat the design on the door of a bathroom cupboard. You could also continue the design around a window.

1 Using a craft knife, score the surface of a piece of waterproof chipboard to provide a key (scuffed surface) for the tiles.

4 Clamp the board firmly and drill the screw holes. Put a drinking straw in each hole to keep them open. Wearing rubber gloves, spread waterproof tile adhesive over about one-third of the board.

2 Seal both sides with diluted PVA (white) glue to prevent it from warping.

3 Plan the design on the board. Mark a point in each corner for the screw holes, for hanging the splashback on the wall.

5 Position the tiles on the board, pressing them firmly into the adhesive. Repeat over the rest of the board, working on one-third of the board at a time. Remove excess adhesive with a damp sponge. Leave to dry.

6 Spread waterproof grout over the surface of the tiles, taking care not to dislodge them. Remove excess with a damp sponge, then polish with a dry, lint-free cloth. Seal the back with two coats of yacht varnish. Mark the screw positions on the wall, and drill and plug them. Screw the board to the wall with chromed mirror screws.

PATTERNED WALL PANEL

lowers have always been a popular theme for tiled wall panels, from the ornate vases of flowers produced at the Iznik potteries in Ottoman Turkey to the blue and white tulip panels made by Delft potters in Holland. Flowers are also a recurring theme in folk art in many countries.

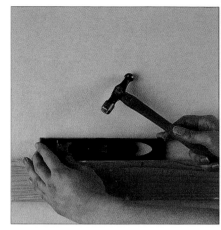

These handmade and hand-painted tiles from the South of France are set directly on to the wall. A border of plain tiles in toning colours makes a perfect frame for the design. You could even edge the tiles with wooden moulding for a picture-frame effect.

1 Prepare the surface of the wall thoroughly. Decide on the position of the panel, then fix two guide battens (furring strips) to the wall.

4 Start to build up the bottom and side of the border with plain tiles. Use tile spacers or space the tiles by eye.

2 Wearing rubber gloves, spread a layer of tile adhesive over the wall between the battens.

3 Using the notched edge of the spreader, key (scuff) the surface of the adhesive.

5 Begin to fill in the space between the bottom and side of the border with the floral tile panel. Continue to build up the panel and border gradually, moving diagonally from the starting point and making sure that the floral panel pieces are properly aligned. Remove excess adhesive with a damp sponge. Leave to dry overnight.

6 Wearing rubber gloves, grout the tiles, pushing the grout down well into the gaps between the tiles. When the grout has set slightly, remove the excess with a damp sponge. When completely dry, polish with a dry, lint-free cloth.

WALL BORDER

These long, star-studded Spanish tiles are a modern version of the tiles made by medieval Islamic potters. They were widely used in place of the more time-consuming tile mosaics that decorate buildings such as the Alhambra Palace in Granada.

Tiles with interconnecting patterns look wonderful as an all-over wall decoration. Here they are used to add a touch of Spanish style in a simple border along the base of a wall.

When using tiles in this manner, bear in mind that they are not designed to take knocks (unless you use thicker worktop or floor tiles), so consider carefully where you will put them.

1 Measure the length of one tile. Using a pencil, mark the wall into sections of this measurement.

4 Using the notched edge of the spreader, key (scuff) the surface only halfway through, leaving a thick layer of adhesive.

2 Using a set square (T-square), draw a vertical line at each mark to help position the tiles accurately.

3 Wearing rubber gloves, spread a thick layer of tile adhesive along the base of the wall. Cover enough wall to apply four or five tiles at a time.

5 Slide each tile into position. You may wish to use tile spacers or you could space them by eye. Wipe the surface of the tiles and the wall with a damp sponge to remove any excess adhesive. Leave to dry.

6 Grout the tiles thoroughly, pushing the grout down well into the gaps between the tiles. Using a damp sponge, remove any excess grout from the surface of the tiles. Use a length of dowel with a rounded end, or a grout shaper, to smooth the grout joint. Leave to dry. Polish the surface of the tiles with a dry, lint-free cloth.

INDEX

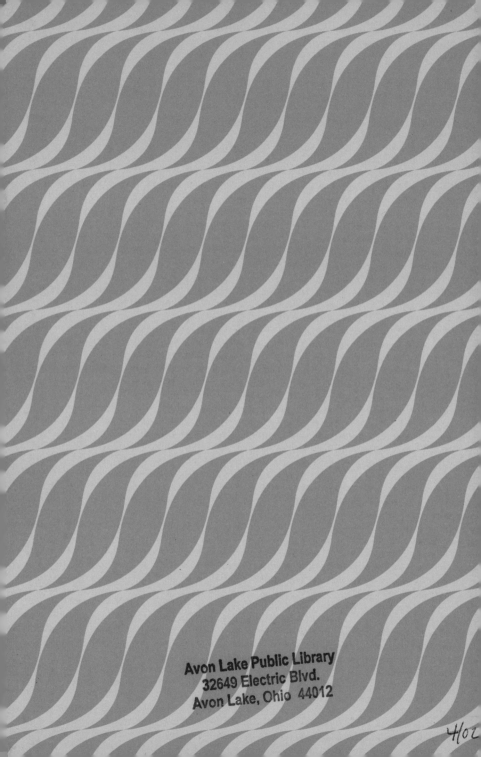

4/02